A CENTURY OF ANARCHY

A CENTURY OF ANARCHY

NEUTRAL MORESNET THROUGH THE REVISIONIST LENS

PETER C. EARLE

10 9 8 7 6 5 4 3 2

ISBN: 978-0-9913059-5-7 (print)
ISBN: 978-0-9913059-4-0 (ebook)

OL25448039M

"When the American spirit was in its youth, the language of America was different: Liberty, sir, was the primary object."
—Patrick Henry

With love to Skyler, Kiersten, Catlin, Megan, and Sean.

Contents

Foreword

THIS WORK is an expansion of an article I wrote in the summer of 2012, and it is the first stand-alone writing about Neutral Moresnet since Charles Hoch's 1882 *The Neutral Territory of Moresnet.*

Moresnet encapsulates the archetype of market anarchy. Hidden in its history we find privately produced, commodity-backed money; competing avenues for the administration of justice; negligible—and, it seems, entirely avoidable—taxes and fees; few, if any, regulations; a defense force without a standing military; open borders (however unintentionally); and an irrepressibly entrepreneurial spirit.

As this work neared completion, a number of individuals who read it asked, "Why a revisionist view? What does it revise?" First, and most broadly, it dismisses the notion that what was happening in a 344-hectare parcel of land for nearly 100 years can be discounted as a mere territorial curiosity or diplomatic fluke. This account also adds to a growing list of documented instances (the American West and the Walled City of Kowloon among them) where, as government dominion waned, liberty and prosperity flourished. Ultimately, the history of Neutral Moresnet assails—convincingly, I believe—the second-worst idea that has ever held mankind in its grasp: that a territorial monopoly on force, a violence warrant, is required for human life to proceed and improve; that the savagery of states is an essential prerequisite for peace and justice.

Thank you for reading.

Peter C. Earle
April 2014

Acknowledgements

EVEN WITH A WORK as short as this one, there are numerous parties to whom gratitude is owed. I wish to mention the scholars and staffers at the Mises Institute in Auburn, Alabama, with whom I've been privileged to share ideas and whose work has added both structure and depth to my apprehensions of liberty. Additional thanks to Jeff Tucker, Doug French, Daniel Brackens, Josep Prat, Dr. Thorsten Polleit, Redmond Weissenberger, Jeff Watson, Jaison De Montalegre, Michelle Ray, and many, many others who've offered friendship alongside their support of my writing and research.

Exceptional thanks are extended to Mike Reid and B. K. Marcus at Invisible Order for their editorial and technical assistance in the process of expanding and executing this composition.

My deepest appreciation—indeed, some degree of indebtedness—goes to Dr. Mary Savage, not only for innumerable rounds of proofreading, but for her tireless encouragement, intellectual stimulation, and moral support.

1. Introduction

COULD A COMMUNITY without a central government avoid descending into chaos and rampant criminality? Could its economy grow and thrive without the intervening regulatory hand of the state? Could disputes between citizens be settled if there existed no state monopoly on legal judgments? Apparently, the answers to these questions are yes, yes, and yes.

Indeed, if the strange and little-known case of the *condominium* of Neutral Moresnet—a tiny wedge of disputed territory in northwestern Europe—acts as our guide, we must conclude that statelessness is not only possible but beneficial to progress, carrying profound advantages over coercive bureaucracies.

The remarkable enterprise that was Moresnet was an unintended consequence of the Napoleonic Wars (1803–1815), which, like all wars, empowered the governments of participating states at the expense of their populations: nationalism grew more fervent, treasuries were depleted, multigenerational levels of debt were incurred, and a new crop of destitute amputees appeared in streets all across Europe.

In the Congress of Vienna, which concluded the war, borders were redrawn according to the "balance of power" theory: no state should be in a position to dominate others militarily. There were some disagreements about the details. One in particular was between Prussia and the Netherlands regarding the miniscule, mineral-rich map spot known as the "old mountain" —*Altenberg* in German, *Vieille Montagne* in French—which held a large zinc mine that profitably extricated tons of ore

1

from the ground. With a major war recently concluded, and the next nearest zinc source of any significance in England, neither of the two powers was willing to give up the area, nor were they eager to fight over it.

So, from its inception in 1816, the zone fell under the joint aegis of several states: Prussia and the Netherlands initially, with Belgium taking the place of the Netherlands after gaining its independence in 1830. Designated "Neutral Moresnet," this small land occupied a triangular spot between those three states. Its area was largely covered by the quarry and a nominal "capital" called Kelmis—consisting of some company buildings, a bank, schools, several stores, a hospital, and 50 or so cottages housing 256 miners and support personnel.[1] Initially, little changed within the district; but over the next few decades, Moresnet's small size and ambiguous oversight by several national powers resulted in an inadvertent experiment deep in the hilly Aachen forests of northwestern Europe.[2]

2. A Prescription for Liberty

WHEN CONSIDERING the unique condition of Neutral Moresnet, two key factors come to the fore. First, it was a mining settlement. Throughout history, small, isolated communities—mining settlements in particular—have typically demonstrated profound propensities toward self-government. As Charles Howard Shinn notes in his 1884 overview,

> everywhere we find, among observers of mining-life, testimony to the system of self-government adopted in the camps.... [R]ecollections are often hazy upon definite points, but they all agree as to the informality

---

1. Robert Shackleton, *Unvisited Places of Old Europe* (Philadelphia: The Penn Publishing Company, 1913), p. 157.

2. Shackleton, 159.

and celerity of early proceedings, and the high degree of good order secured in every camp, without exception.[3]

Richard J. Ogelsby, Governor of Illinois from 1865 to 1869, was himself a mining speculator in the American Old West; he wrote that there was "very little law, but a large amount of good order" and that "crime was rare, for punishment was certain."[4]

Additionally, the terrain of the area within which the tiny colony was located was mountainous. Situated at the intersection of the Netherlands, Belgium, and Prussia—the *dreilandenpunt* (three-land point)—at an elevation of nearly 1,000 feet, the Moresnet territory sits largely on the downslope into an extremely fertile, productive valley.[5] Elevated lands, from Ancient Greece to the central highlands of Vietnam, have long been associated with the inspiration to self-rule. As Erik von Kuehnelt-Leddhin wrote in 1943,

> the headway which egalitarianism and [xenophobic nationalism] made after the revolutions of 1830 and 1848 is intimately connected with the rapid increase of two geographical-social units. Europe of the nineteenth and beginning twentieth century [became] a continent ruled by money, and money comes from the rich *plains* and the *cities*.[6]

He adds that

> "Historical" Europe ... is mountainous ... [and we find] "real" Europe in the mountaineers. In these parts of the world traditions have been better preserved; patriarchalism,

---

3. Charles Howard Shinn, *Mining Camps: A Study in Frontier Government* (New York: Charles Scribner's Sons, 1884), p. 164–165.

4. Shinn, 160.

5. Charles Hoch, *The Neutral Territory of Moresnet* (Cambridge: The Riverside Press, 1882), p. 5.

6. Erik von Kuehnelt-Leddhin, *The Menace of the Herd* (Milwaukee: The Bruce Publishing Company, 1943), p. 126.

piety, loyalty, altruism—all the truly "romantic" virtues are here more at home than on the progressive plains.... [M]ountain culture is not "advanced" ... [yet] serfdom practically never existed among the mountaineers. The mountains were essentially free. "Freedom thrives in the mountains," Schiller exclaims justly. Yet it is also interesting to see how violently the mountain peasant was attacked by urban writers in the second half of the nineteenth century, attacked and vilified for his loyalty to traditions. Having no social grievances ... he was the very despair of urban, leftist agitators.[7]

Mountains, of course, are difficult to ascend, perilous to traverse, and often offer initial settlers little arable or otherwise productive land. Therefore, those who successfully occupy and tame such lands—which are secluded, inhospitable, or both— tend to be independent in both lifestyle and mind, having earned their place due to self-sufficiency. Historically, they are resistant to change, and consequently, they do not readily accept outside authority.

3. Prosperity in Seclusion

STONE BORDER MARKERS delineating the borders of the neutral territory—some of which still stand today—were emplaced in 1818. But although nominally monitored by several nations, by virtue of its small size Moresnet was loosely supervised at best; a crumb would easily blot out its very existence on most maps. In fact, on many Prussian maps, the triangular parcel was omitted entirely. Neither was there much reason for its overseers to direct attention to it: it sat quietly, reliably excavating 8,500 tons of zinc each year. Occasionally a patrolling Prussian, Dutch, or Belgian soldier would wander close to the border—as a demilitarized zone, Moresnet was explicitly off

---

7. Kuehnelt-Leddhin, 127.

4

limits for military forces—but for the most part, the mining community was left alone.

And it wasn't just administrators who lost track of the anomalous territory. The place was secluded enough that one traveler "recalled inquiring at [a nearby] hotel, at some neighboring shops, and at both of the railway stations ... [but still couldn't be told] how to reach Neutral Moresnet; they had no idea at all, or guessed at random at various impossible stations."[8] Fifty years after Moresnet's establishment, a baffled stamp-collecting periodical noted, "We confess we are but half enlightened as to its whereabouts."[9]

Within the triangle, there was a minimal government in the form of a burgomaster, assisted by a "Committee of Ten." Despite its somewhat-ominous name, the committee "wield[ed] no real power" and the burgomaster was "far from being a ... despot."[10]

From establishment to occupation, Neutral Moresnet had four burgomasters. With the exception of one who lasted three months—there is likely a fascinating story there, now lost to history—on average they held that title for 32 years (much unlike democracy's revolving door). And from 1882 to 1885, Moresnet didn't have a burgomaster at all.

Burgomasters, 1817–1915

Arnold Timothée de Lasaulx: 1817–February 2, 1859 (42 years)
Adolf Hubert van Scherpenzeel-Thim: February 2–May 30, 1859 (3 months)
Joseph Kohl: June 1, 1859–February 3, 1882 (23 years)
Vacancy: 1882–1885 (three years without any governance)
Hubert Schmetz: June 20, 1885–March 15, 1915 (30 years)[11]

Moresnet also employed a police force of one, referred to with local good humor—and perhaps mockery of nearby Prussia with its General Staff and large social class of military

---

8. Shackleton, 159.

9. "Newly-issued or Inedited Stamps," *The Stamp-Collector's Magazine* Vol V, May 1, 1867.

10. Ibid, 161. 11. Schmetz's term was followed by the German occupation.

officers—as Moresnet's "Secretary of War."[12] The lone police officer was usually "to be seen in full uniform enjoying a game of chess or billiards with the burgomaster at the beer garden on the shores of the lake."[13]

Through the remainder of the nineteenth century, Moresnet's course ran apart from those of surrounding European states. In 1848, for example, violent revolutions broke out in Italy, France, Germany, Denmark, Hungary, Switzerland, Poland, Ireland, Wallachia, the Ukraine, and throughout the Habsburg Empire. For Moresnetians, life in 1848 proceeded unperturbed, and the year was noteworthy only for the first minting of sovereign coins, which local merchants could accept for use alongside other currencies.[14] Even if the ideas underlying the waves of dissent—socialism and nationalism—had reached Moresnet, it doesn't seem likely that they would have resonated with an essentially stateless community.

Over the decades of its independence, the population of the tiny, peaceful region grew accordingly: by 1850, the number of inhabitants had doubled, and in addition to the zinc mine, new businesses and even some small farms began to spring up. The population of the hamlet then quadrupled between 1850 and 1860, topping 2,000 residents. Despite Moresnet's isolation, word slowly spread that within Moresnet—if one could find it—"imports from surrounding countries were toll free, the taxes were very low, prices were lower and wages higher than in [other European] countries."[15]

Along with the negligible tax burden, a unique legal climate favored the expansion of economic activity within the tiny district. On inception, the Congress of Vienna, which created Neutral Moresnet, held that its laws would be construed in accordance with the *Code Napoleon*, known for "its stress on

---

12. "Europe's Smallest State" *New York Times* October 31, 1886.

13. Shackleton, 164.   14. "Coins," Moresnet.nl.

15. "Life in Neutral Moresnet," Moresnet.nl.

clearly written and accessible law, [which] was a major step in replacing the previous patchwork of feudal laws." Furthermore, "laws could be applied only if they had been duly promulgated, and only if they had been published officially (including provisions for publishing delays, given the means of communication available at the time); thus no secret laws were authorized. It [also] prohibited ex post facto laws."[16]

Most importantly of all, the Code Napoleon placed primary importance on "property rights … [which] were made absolute," naturally generating a favorable climate for commercial enterprise.[17] One periodical noted that a "thief tried … [nearby] gets … a few months, while the Code Napoleon specifies five years."[18]

The efficiency and transparency of the Code Napoleon contrasted sharply with the *Allgemeines Landrecht* legal system of neighboring Prussia, which "used an incredibly casuistic and imprecise language, making it hard to properly understand and use in practice." However, for some legal purposes, the Landrecht system may have held advantages over the Code Napoleon, and the residents of Moresnet may have used it when it suited them for a given case.[19]

Alternatively, disputes could be directed to the burgomaster's "petty tribunal" for quick decisions on smaller issues and disputes.[20]

> His head-quarters were … "under his hat." He went about town and held court wherever he happened to be when his service as justice was required, which, happily, was not often. When complaint was made to him, he

16. "Napoleonic Code," Wikipedia.org.

17. "The Civil Code," Napoleon-Series.org.

18. Naval Intelligence Division, *A Manual of Belgium and the Adjoining Territories.* (Great Britain: H. M. Stationary Office, 1918) p. 246.

19. "General state laws for the Prussian states," Wikipedia.org.

20. Shackleton, 166.

would listen patiently and attentively ... [then] whistle some favorite air, and thus take time to revolve the matter in his mind.... His judgments were always intelligible and fair, insomuch that they were never excepted to or appealed from during all his term of thirty-five years.[21]

Moresnet inhabitants, therefore, had access to several different systems for resolution of disputes—the burgomaster's on-the-spot deliberation, the Code Napoleon, and the Landrecht system. Thus, they were served by a rudimentary market for justice, and were therefrom empowered to take their issues to the venue they felt afforded the best chances of satisfactory resolution.

Further, residents of Neutral Moresnet were not required to fulfill the compulsory military requirements of their nations of origin.[22] This is not to say that Moresnet was without military potential of its own. If edifice is evidence, one of the most popular organizations among citizens of Moresnet was the rifle club, which was contained within a "great hall." It is not inconceivable that a secondary purpose of this organization was irregular territorial defense. Regardless, the freedom from the obligation to participate in national armies no doubt motivated many of the new arrivals—in particular those from Prussia, which fought half a dozen wars during the nineteenth century.[23]

One newcomer was particularly significant. Dr. Wilhelm Molly arrived in 1863 to become the general practitioner of the mining company, and soon won celebrity by thwarting a local cholera epidemic in Moresnet. Like many physicians of his era, Dr. Molly was polymathic and had numerous interests, from

---

21. William S. Walsh, *A Handy Book of Curious Information* (Philadelphia: J. B. Lippincott Company, 1913), p. 558–559.

22. Both Belgium (1847) and Prussia (1875) ultimately rescinded their exemption of emigrants in the Moresnet zone from military conscription.

23. "List of wars 1800–1899," Wikipedia.org.

business and politics to science and linguistics, the lattermost of which would play a pivotal role in Moresnet's later years.[24]

From the beginning of the designation of Neutral Moresnet, it was known that the Vieille Montagne zinc mine could not, and would not, produce indefinitely. In 1885, the zinc mine finally wound down and ceased operation, but this wasn't especially worrisome economically: numerous businesses were now flourishing, including "60–70 bars and cafes [along] the main street," small farms, and at least one dairy operation.[25] A number of tiny breweries and brandy distilleries functioned, filling the bottles and casks of Moresnet's establishments, as well as providing inventory for local smugglers. Taxes hadn't changed since the designation of the neutral zone in 1816, and visitors noted that Moresnet was "without the beggars who are [a] sadly familiar sight" across the rest of Europe.[26] Indeed,

> at the date of the treaty it contained only a few barracks and a trifling population. Now the joint effects of liberty and industry are seen in the increase of the inhabitants [and] the people live in a happy state of insignificance.[27]

To Dr. Molly, the closing of the zinc mine hardly presented a reason to expect the decline of Neutral Moresnet as a community, much less its end. On the contrary, he became the foremost advocate of pursuing a path of complete independence and severing the few ties that Moresnet had with Prussia and Belgium. Within a year after the zinc mine closed down, he spearheaded the founding of a local, private postal service—

---

24. The Moresnet.nl website notes that Wilhelm Molly was awarded the *Geheimrat* title by Prussia, which translates to "special [medical] counselor." This author finds amusement in noting that the term may have incurred ironic gravity over time, as it was also used by German kaisers to refer to academics that irritated them, as Molly's heroic efforts to acquire complete Moresnetian independence undoubtedly did.

25. "Life in Neutral Moresnet," Moresnet.nl.   26. Shackleton, 171.

27. *The Stamp-Collector's Magazine* Vol V, May 1, 1867.

but within 17 days after its founding it was discovered and shut down by Prussian and Belgian authorities. Undeterred, he explored numerous other initiatives.

In 1903, a group of entrepreneurs proposed developing a casino in Moresnet to rival those in Monte Carlo, offering to build electric trolleys to nearby towns and "share the profit with every citizen."[28] In fact, a small casino opened briefly, but like the postal service it was short-lived; on hearing of it, the king of Belgium threatened Moresnet's always-tenuous independence.

4. The Esperantist Initiative

BUT BELGIUM proved the least of Moresnet's worries. In 1900 the Prussian state—now itself consolidated into a greater German Empire—began to undertake "aggressive" tactics toward pressuring the residents of the zone to consent to absorption.[29] True to that country's martial heritage, Prussian efforts included "outright sabotage," such as cutting off Moresnet's electricity and telephone connections.[30] When citizens attempted to run new electrical and telephone lines, Prussia tried to thwart them. (Prussia also apparently took steps toward "prevent[ing] the appointment of new … officials" known to support Moresnetian independence.[31])

One might ask what a miniscule community, centered on a depleted zinc mine and absent from most maps, could possibly have offered Germany, but such a question ignores the animating principle of states: to accumulate and wield power. Europe in the early part of the nineteenth century was rife with "shreds and patches" of independence. Moresnet was among

---

28. "The Smallest in Europe," *New York Times* September 28, 1905.
29. "How It Ended," Moresnet.nl.
30. Ibid.
31. Ibid.

the last remnants of these.[32] Holdouts against the rising tide of state consolidation frankly embarrassed "men like Bismarck [and Garibaldi, in Italy, who] had won institutional prestige by adopting uniform standards and eliminating exceptions. Progress was supposed to mean the end of the latter."[33]

Nevertheless, "the Moresnetians, small though their territory, w[ould] not be cabined, cribbed, confined."[34] Despite increasing harassment by a state thousands of times larger and armed to the teeth, by 1907 the population of the hamlet had increased to almost 3,800, only 460 of whom were descendants of the original Moresnetians.[35] The rest came from varied and far-flung locations: these people were not only Germans, Belgians, and Hollanders, but also former residents of Italy, Switzerland, and Russia—eventually there were also two Americans and even one Chinese resident. A large cathedral had come to occupy the center of the community, which had expanded to over 800 homes.[36] Even though Belgian Aix-la-Chapelle was nearby and offered a more cosmopolitan experience, in general, the Moresnetians chose "not [to] leave the Triangle, but variedly find the spice of life within its slender borders."[37]

---

32. Discussion of the smaller states in Europe typically steers toward Andorra, Monaco, Monte Carlo, or Liechtenstein, but many far smaller, Moresnet-like communities existed, legacies of the post-feudal era. Several are particularly fascinating: A now-submerged island in the Danube River was once known as "No One's Island," hosting a Turkish community who were free from customs, taxes, and conscription. Another island, the five-mile-long Tavolara, sat in the Mediterranean, home to 70 citizens. In the virtually inaccessible peaks of the Pyrenees, the settlement of St. Goust was ruled for centuries by a "council of elders." Today, we find honorable successors to these autonomous communities in such physical territories as the Principalities of Hutt River (in Australia) and Seborga (in Italy), and virtual communities including social networks and cryptoeconomies.

33. Steven Michael Press, "To Govern, or Not to Govern: Prussia, Neutral Moresnet" on SSRN.com, June 29, 2010.

34. Shackleton, 172.   35. Ibid, 157.   36. "The Smallest in Europe," *New York Times* September 28, 1905.   37. Shackleton, 163.

Dr. Molly—now having lived in "thoroughly autonomous" Neutral Moresnet for half a century—began to view the independence and prosperity of Moresnet as a place compatible with the *Weltanschauung* of one of his intellectual pursuits: the universal language and culture of Esperanto.[38] While a detailed discussion of Esperanto is beyond the scope of this writing, the synthetic language was founded in 1887 by L. L. Zamenhof to eliminate the "hate and prejudice" that he theorized arose between ethnic groups owing to language differences and often led to war; and it should come as little surprise that Esperanto's founder additionally expressed his

> profound [conviction] that every nationalism offers humanity only the greatest unhappiness.... It is true that the nationalism of oppressed peoples—as a natural self-defensive reaction—is much more excusable than the nationalism of peoples who oppress; but, if the nationalism of the strong is ignoble, the nationalism of the weak is imprudent; both give birth to and support each other.[39]

Espousing this thinly veiled antistate philosophy, and having corresponded for years with prominent Esperantists around the world, in 1906 Dr. Molly met with several colleagues to

---

38. Links between anarchism/libertarianism and Esperanto are copious, if perplexingly under-investigated. While a portion of Esperanto's usage has always been co-opted by leftist and Utopian groups, its founding principle was antistate to the extent that it was created to skirt nationalism and provide possibilities for more seamless, peaceful interaction: facilitating trade and avoiding violent conflict. The great writer and linguistic genius J. R. R. Tolkien, who occasionally espoused antistate views ("My political opinions lean more and more to anarchy. The most improper job of any man, even saints, is bossing other men.") wrote, "My advice to all who have the time or inclination to concern themselves with the international language movement would be: 'Back Esperanto loyally.'" See "La Filozofio de Libereco" ("The Philosophy of Liberty"), ISIL.org.

39. N. Z. Maimon, "La Cionista Periodo en la Vivo de Zamenhof," *Nica Literatura Revuo* 3/5: p. 165–177.

discuss designating Neutral Moresnet as a self-determining global haven for Esperantists—a territory that would "embrace aims and ideals affecting the brotherhood of man ... [and] civilized life ... emancipating ourselves from all that is absurd and unworthy in convention, all that the ignorant centuries have imposed upon us."[40] As part of that initiative, he proposed that the name of the enclave be changed to *Amikejo*—Esperanto for "place of friendship." This name not only espoused the Moresnetians (or Amikejans) explicitly peaceful nature, but undoubtedly thrust a propagandistic thumb into the eye of ever-marauding Prussia. Two years later, in 1908, a large celebration was held commemorating the launch of the renamed Amikejo, complete with festivities and the airing of a new national anthem.[41] Unsurprisingly, the occasion went unnoted (and Amikejo unrecognized) by nearby states, although numerous newspapers reported the event. To this day, some buildings in Kelmis still bear the large green star that is the symbol of Esperanto.

Two early projects planned to draw both commercial and recreational interest: the establishment of an International Chamber of Commerce and an annual theatre festival. Neither, regrettably, saw realization.

By 1914, Amikejo's population topped 4,600 people, peacefully cohabiting in an economically prosperous political limbo characterized by an "absence of definite rule."[42] Signs and notifications were printed in German, French, and Esperanto, and residents had developed one of the "queerest and most unintelligible dialects in the world."[43] Indeed, an American— an American of the turn of the century, no less—described

40. "An Esperanto City," *The Strand Magazine* Vol XXXVI, No. 215 (1908): 559.

41. The anthem performed at the founding of Amikejo can be heard at http://moresnet.nl/images/volkslied/marsprt1.mp3.

42. Shackleton, 165.   43. "Neutral Moresnet," *New York Times* May 10, 1919.

the community as having "a sort of *al fresco* freedom of life, an untrammelledness which comes naturally from long-continued absence of centralized restraint."[44]

Indeed; for a century, residents and settlers in the diminutive wedge of land had found governments—internal and foreign—superfluous to and inimical toward the attainment of individual liberty. In one sense the Moresnet/Amikejo experiment might be viewed as Europe's analog to the American West, covering a greater length of time but on an infinitesimally smaller scale.

One reporter described it as follows:

> One of the smallest and strangest territories in the world ... an encircling ridge of high mountains veritably buries it from neighboring civilization and culture and leaves it in a little world of its own.... [And] for nearly a century, the inhabitants have never experienced the feeling of being under the rule of an emperor, king or president. They are independent, governed by no one, at liberty to do as they please.[45]

More to the point, another visitor described Amikejo in simple terms: "a legal anarchy."[46]

5. War, Hunger, and Negation

DESPITE A VIBRANT, small-scale economy, the existence of the district remained enormously fragile in the tempestuous political environment of early twentieth-century continental Europe. Amikejans perennially worried over the "impermanency of their pleasing status," and this concern was realized in 1914 when war broke out between France and Germany.[47]

---

44. Shackleton, 173.

45. "Neutral Territory of Moresnet," *Sausalito News* January 23, 1915: p. 3.

46. Louis Viereck, "Moresnet—The Smallest State on Earth," *The Fatherland* Vol III, No. 2 (1915): 33.

47. Shackleton, 173.

There exist two starkly contradicting accounts of Amikejo's experience in the opening of World War I. The Victorian adventurer George Clark Musgrave wrote of the German onslaught that, while "the pretty towns defended near the [Belgian] frontier were soon flaming ruins, the quaint neutral territory of Moresnet [was] an oasis in a desert of destruction."[48] Unless Musgrave's benign description was made exclusively with respect to property damage, it is difficult to reconcile his account with that of Flor O'Squarr:

> The neutral territory of Moresnet was violated by the Germans on the morning of August 1st, 1914.... Soldiers crossed the frontier and occupied the 850 acres, whilst an officer scattered the councilors and took possession of the town hall.... Two hundred inhabitants of Belgian origin were torn from their homes and taken as prisoners to Germany. A Dutchman and a Moresnetian were shot on the pretext that they resisted the Army of Occupation. After this a proclamation was put up giving notice to the rest of the inhabitants that they were henceforward Germans.[49]

The suspicion that "Prussia ... always had the intention to appropriate the territory" was confirmed when Germany statutorily annexed the district in 1915.[50] Access to Moresnet, once characterized largely by the difficulty of finding it, became an arduous, bureaucratic undertaking; in a passage adumbrative of the world to come in the wake of the Great War, one journalist explains that

> to reach Moresnet we journeyed by automobile from Liege for about two hours to some beautiful districts

---

48. George Clarke Musgrave, *Under Four Flags for France* (New York: D. Appleton & Co., 1918), p. 8.

49. Ch. Flor O'Squarr, "The Neutrality of Moresnet," *The Contemporary Review* No. 613 (1917): 248. O'Squarr was an unknown pseudonymous author.

50. "The Defence and Military Service," Moresnet.nl.

in the Ardennes, mounting gradually higher until at last on the opposite side of a little stream the black and white striped bars announced that we had reached the border.... We stopped and showed our passports. The English-speaking German officer objected that they were not vised for Prussian territory. On telling him that we were on a tour of inspection and did not desire to enter Prussian territory, he explained that to reach Moresnet... we would have to cross about 12 feet of Prussian soil. We found that by climbing a fence we could reach the country without invading Prussia. The officer, however, objected, and at last we discovered that half of the road was neutral, while the other half was Prussian. We offered to keep the automobile on the wrong side of the road and thus evade the Prussian territory. After a long wait occupied with much telephoning we were permitted to cross the 12 feet of Prussian territory with unvised passports, provided a German officer was in attendance.[51]

Indeed, the degree of fixity of borders seems to be an indicator of how fully state power has permeated a region. Needless to say, severe limits on both individual movement and trade with the district crushed Moresnet's economy. A community once praised for its "liberty and industry"

began to suffer for a lack of food.... [It] was not German, therefore the Germans refused to feed the Belgians while the latter refused to admit food to feed the Germans.[52]

Relief issues were also complicated by the obvious lack of nationalist fervor, when

an effort was made to separate the [Germans and Belgians within Moresnet], but they were found so mixed, living

---

51. "Newest Neutral Country is Found," *The Spokesman-Review* January 16, 1916: p. 12.
52. Ibid.

in the same house, members of the same family and many speaking the same tongue, that any separation was impossible.[53]

Ultimately, food aid was sent by both German and Belgian authorities.

By 1918, with the end of the war in sight, the *Contemporary Review*, a British journal of politics and social reform, considered the impending plight of Amikejo, née Moresnet:

The fate of Moresnet has been forgotten in this immense catastrophe. We must bear it in mind. After the victory the plenipotentiaries who draw up the conditions of peace must not neglect this poor little piece of independence which has been victimized.[54]

A more impassioned plea in defense of the autonomous "shreds and patches" of Europe was taken up by journalist Archer P. Whallon. Ending a defense of the "anarchy of nations" consisting of numerous communities "tucked away in odd corners" or "inhospitable mountain-ranges in Europe" by citing Moresnet, he concludes that

with the breaking up of the old political structures of Austria-Hungary and of Russia, there have been heard the pleas of several small communities of peoples, distinct in race and customs from the peoples that surround them, for independence.... They are political curiosities that mankind can well afford to protect.[55]

It was not to be. Sometime in 1919, a sign appeared in Kelmis, roughly translating to

Inhabitants of Moresnet! Adorn the houses! Put up flags! Peace has come! Moresnet has disappeared from the map! Belgium, which in difficult times shielded us, is

53. Ibid.   54. O'Squarr.   55. Archer P. Whallon, "Nations That Never Grew Up," *St. Nicholas* Vol XLVI, No. 11 (1919): 1005.

17

to be our homeland! What was meant to be 25 years ago has found its realization.[56]

Details pertaining to the official turnover followed.

The costs of the Great War were unimaginably staggering, dwarfing those of previous conflicts in virtually every category: 37 million casualties, the influenza pandemic, widespread hunger, civil dislocation, and economic wreckage. Yet another crop of destitute, sometimes uniformed, amputees appeared in the streets of devastated European cities. But another, seldom-considered consequence of the war—of all wars—was and remains those uncountable heaps of unfulfilled promises and discarded goals left in the wake of the conflagration. And with a mere 16 words, Article 32 of the Treaty of Versailles— "Germany recognizes the full sovereignty of Belgium over the whole of the contested territory of Moresnet"[57]—a century of self-determination ended.

Despite ten decades of putative anarchy in Moresnet, the violence, disorder, and wreckage typically attributed to state-lessness arrived only when governments did.

6. A Century of Anarchy

FOR ITS BRIEF CENTURY of accidental autonomy, Moresnet demonstrated the possibilities that statelessness holds out for peace, prosperity, and good order. Without an army, it was at peace. Without heavy taxation, import/export controls, or other economic regulations, it was prosperous. Without a central authority over legal disputes and without a police force larger than a single chess player, it was shockingly free of crime. At the turn of the century, when chattel slavery and

---

56. http://moresnet.nl/images/geschiedenis/friede.jpg

57. "The Versailles Treaty June 28, 1919: Part III," The Avalon Project, Yale Law School.

institutionalized discrimination were common in many parts of the world, individuals of several languages and races peacefully inhabited Moresnet's stone-traced borders.

But let us not allow the end of Moresnet, nor the ease of its conquest, suggest that stateless enclaves or other microstates are either destined to fail or inherently flawed. Rather, let us reflect on the hundred years of unplanned social peace and economic progress inside its "slender borders," ended only by the intrusion of the warring nation-states that had for a time forgotten it. The suppression of Moresnet's experiment in statelessness bears witness to the intolerable power that states had then acquired at the beginning of the twentieth century, and today far surpass at the dawning of the twenty-first.

About the Author

PETER C. EARLE is the owner of Intangible Economics LLC†, a consultancy focusing on game economy design, monetization, virtual goods, and digital/cryptocurrencies. In addition to designing and managing the economies of a number of global, massively multiplayer online games and serving as the Chief Economist of Humint (a cryptocurrency advisory firm) he has spent nineteen years in trading and management roles with hedge funds and proprietary trading firms.

Pete regularly publishes articles on economic history, free markets, and spontaneous order. He is a graduate of the United States Military Academy, has an MBA, and is currently engaged in further graduate studies in Applied Economics at American University and in Data Science through the Bloomberg School of Public Health at Johns Hopkins University.

Contact Pete at pete.earle@gmail.com.

---

† www.intangibleeconomics.com